FOR EVERYTHING A SEASON

A 30-Day Ecclesiastes Journal

Friendship Press®

Friendship Press
P.O. Box 117
Wyncote, PA 19095

Library of Congress Catalog-in-Publication data available upon request

ISBN (hardcover): 978-1-961088-14-6

Verse selection and prompts by Scott Tunseth
Cover and interior design by Laurie Ingram

Typesetting by Integra Software Services Pvt. Ltd.
Printed in the United States of America

About This Journal

Each *NRSVue Bible Journal* is offered with the hope that you will be inspired by your encounter with scripture and that journaling becomes a helpful part of your devotional journey.

The undated pages allow you to write at your own pace, with scripture passages and thoughtful writing prompts placed at regular intervals for you to meditate on, pray over, and write about as the Spirit moves you.

The book of Ecclesiastes has comforted and challenged readers for centuries and in this volume, thirty of the most impactful passages from this timeless text are presented for your reflection. The writing prompts will help you think about how to apply this wisdom in your life today. May the Teacher's musings be a light on your path.

date

Ecclesiastes 1:2-4

Vanity of vanities, says the Teacher,
  vanity of vanities! All is vanity.
What do people gain from all the toil
  at which they toil under the sun?
A generation goes, and a generation comes,
  but the earth remains forever.

date

The ancient royal philosopher who authored the book of Ecclesiastes poses a challenging question about human existence. How might you answer the philosopher's question regarding toil? What makes your work meaningful, or not?

date

ECCLESIASTES 1:9-10

What has been is what will be,
  and what has been done is what will be done;
  there is nothing new under the sun.
Is there a thing of which it is said,
  "See, this is new"?
It has already been
  in the ages before us.

date

The royal philosopher suggests that nothing which happens is really new. How comfortable are you with such a thought? Why?

date

date

date

ECCLESIASTES 1:17-18

And I applied my mind to know wisdom and to know madness and folly.
I perceived that this also is but a chasing after wind.
For in much wisdom is much vexation,
and those who increase knowledge increase sorrow.

date

Wisdom is usually considered a good thing, including in the Bible. Reflect on the royal philosopher's take on wisdom in these verses. Have you experienced "knowing too much"?

date

date

date

ECCLESIASTES 2:13-14

Then I saw that wisdom excels folly as light excels darkness.

The wise have eyes in their head,

  but fools walk in darkness.

Yet I perceived that the same fate befalls all of them.

date

Describe a time when you had the eyes of wisdom. Recall a time when being foolish took you to a dark place.

date

ECCLESIASTES 2:18-19

I hated all my toil in which I had toiled under the sun, seeing that I must leave it to my successor, and who knows whether he will be wise or foolish? Yet he will be master of all for which I toiled and used my wisdom under the sun. This also is vanity.

date

The royal philosopher doesn't like the idea of leaving his work in the hands of a successor. Reflect on a time you left a job or retired and had to leave the work in the hands of another? How did you feel? Were your feelings justified or not?

date

date

date

ECCLESIASTES 3:1-2

For everything there is a season and a time for every matter under heaven:
a time to be born and a time to die;
a time to plant and a time to pluck up what is planted;
a time to kill and a time to heal;
a time to break down and a time to build up;

date

How would you describe the "season" you are in right now? Is it stormy, balmy, barren, or breezy? Do you need a change of seasons? Why or why not?

date

date

date

ECCLESIASTES 3:1, 3

For everything there is a season and a time for every matter under heaven:
a time to kill and a time to heal;
a time to break down and a time to build up;

date

What may need to die (metaphorically) or be killed in your life? What may need to be healed or built up? Imagine how will this happen?

date

ECCLESIASTES 3:1, 4

For everything there is a season and a time for every matter under heaven:
A time to weep and a time to laugh;
a time to mourn and a time to dance;

date

Recall a time you cried. What were your tears telling you? Describe what brings you joy?

date

date

date

ECCLESIASTES 3:1, 8

For everything there is a season and a time for every matter under heaven:
a time to love and a time to hate;
a time for war and a time for peace.

date

Consider how love and peace coexist with hate and war in God's world. Why is this so? What is your prayer for peace?

date

date

date

ECCLESIASTES 3:9, 12-14

What gain have the workers from their toil?
I know that there is nothing better for them than to be happy and enjoy themselves as long as they live; moreover, it is God's gift that all should eat and drink and take pleasure in all their toil. I know that whatever God does endures forever; nothing can be added to it nor anything taken from it; God has done this so that all should stand in awe before him.

date

Describe how these words are true in your life. What makes you happy, or what dampens your happiness?

date

ECCLESIASTES 4:9-12

Two are better than one because they have a good reward for their toil. For if they fall, one will lift up the other, but woe to one who is alone and falls and does not have another to help. Again, if two lie together, they keep warm, but how can one keep warm alone? And though one might prevail against another, two will withstand one. A threefold cord is not quickly broken.

date

Compose a note of thanks to one who has lifted you up or continues to lift you up. If you are feeling alone or lonely, describe what you need.

date

date

date

ECCLESIASTES 5:2-3

Never be rash with your mouth nor let your heart be quick to utter a word before God, for God is in heaven and you upon earth; therefore let your words be few.

For dreams come with many cares, and a fool's voice with many words.

date

What rings true about the philosopher's words? Recall a time you spoke rashly or a time you spoke with measured wisdom. What were the consequences?

date

date

date

ECCLESIASTES 5:10

The lover of money will not be satisfied with money, nor the lover of wealth with gain. This also is vanity.

date

Why does loving money or wealth often not result in deep personal satisfaction? Reflect on why this is true generally, or perhaps true for you. Describe the non-monetary things that satisfy you most.

date

ECCLESIASTES 5:18-19

This is what I have seen to be good: it is fitting to eat and drink and find enjoyment in all the toil with which one toils under the sun the few days of the life God gives us, for this is our lot. Likewise, all to whom God gives wealth and possessions and whom he enables to enjoy them and to accept their lot and find enjoyment in their toil—this is the gift of God.

date

Imagine your life as a wrapped gift from God. When you open the package what do you find?

date

date

date

ECCLESIASTES 6:10-12

Whatever has come to be has already been named, and it is known what humans are and that they are not able to dispute with those who are stronger. The more words, the more vanity, so how is one the better? For who knows what is good for mortals while they live the few days of their vain life, which they pass like a shadow? For who can tell them what will be after them under the sun?

date

The royal philosopher of Ecclesiastes often seems to think that what happens in life is pre-determined, or what we might call "fate." Does this ring true for you, or not? Why?

date

date

date

ECCLESIASTES 7:3-4

Sorrow is better than laughter,
 for by sadness of countenance the heart is made glad.
The heart of the wise is in the house of mourning,
 but the heart of fools is in the house of mirth.

date

It seems that the royal philosopher has become disillusioned with life, or at least prefers to swim in the streams of sadness rather than the waters of joy. Recount a time you preferred feelings of sadness to celebrating. Describe the waters in which you currently swim.

date

ECCLESIASTES 7:5-6, 11-12

It is better to hear the rebuke of the wise
 than to hear the song of fools.
For like the crackling of thorns under a pot,
 so is the laughter of fools;
 this also is vanity.

Wisdom is as good as an inheritance,
 an advantage to those who see the sun.
For the protection of wisdom is like the protection of money,
 and the advantage of knowledge is that wisdom gives life to the one who possesses it.

date

Where do you see or hear the crackling thorns of foolishness in the world? What wisdom do you wish the world would more readily embrace?

date

date

date

ECCLESIASTES 7:9

Do not be quick to anger,
for anger lodges in the bosom of fools.

date

How has this passage been true for you? If you are angry about something right now, describe it. Imagine how you will dislodge it from your mind and spirit.

date

date

date

ECCLESIASTES 8:11-14

Because sentence against an evil deed is not executed speedily, the human heart is fully set to do evil. Though sinners do evil a hundred times and prolong their lives, yet I know that it will be well with those who fear God, because they stand in fear before him, but it will not be well with the wicked, neither will they prolong their days like a shadow, because they do not stand in fear before God.

There is a vanity that takes place on earth, that there are righteous people who are treated according to the conduct of the wicked and wicked people who are treated according to the conduct of the righteous. I said that this also is vanity.

date

This passage wrestles with the idea that evil people sometimes seem to succeed in life, or at least escape immediate punishment, while the righteous sometimes suffer. How would you talk with God about your own experience of life's "fairness"?

date

ECCLESIASTES 8:15

So I commend enjoyment, for there is nothing better for people under the sun than to eat and drink and enjoy themselves, for this will go with them in their toil through the days of life that God gives them under the sun.

date

The royal philosopher returns to the theme of enjoying life while we can. How comfortable are you with this idea? Describe what brings you joy. If joy and faith intersect for you, express how this happens.

date

date

date

ECCLESIASTES 9:1

All this I laid to heart, examining it all, how the righteous and the wise and their deeds are in the hand of God; whether it is love or hate one does not know.

date

The deeds of the wise and righteous are in God's hands, but "whether it is love or hate" is a mysterious reference. What are your thoughts about this? Then recount a time you felt your deeds were in God's hands.

date

date

date

ECCLESIASTES 9:11-12

Again I saw that under the sun the race is not to the swift, nor the battle to the strong, nor bread to the wise, nor riches to the intelligent, nor favor to the skillful, but time and chance happen to them all. For no one can anticipate one's time. Like fish taken in a cruel net or like birds caught in a snare, so mortals are snared at a time of calamity, when it suddenly falls upon them.

date

This passage upends the conventional understanding of the rewards of swiftness, strength, wisdom, intelligence, or skillfulness. Why? Because eventually those who possess such things face the same fate as everyone else. Do you agree or disagree with this perspective?

date

ECCLESIASTES 10:1-2

Dead flies make the perfumer's ointment give off a foul odor;
so a little folly outweighs wisdom and honor.
The heart of the wise inclines to the right,
but the heart of a fool to the left.

date

Even something as small as one dead fly can ruin the smell of a batch of perfume. Write some other analgies to describe the impact of foolish talk or action. If you have ever experienced this, describe the incident and how it felt.

date

date

date

ECCLESIASTES 10:12-15

Words spoken by the wise bring them favor,
  but the lips of fools consume them.
The words of their mouths begin in foolishness,
  and their talk ends in wicked madness,
yet fools talk on and on.
  No one knows what is to happen,
  and who can tell anyone what the future holds?
The toil of fools wears them out,
  for they do not even know the way to town.

date

What are your sources of wisdom? Who has made a wise difference in your life? Have you ever been "lost" in foolishness? How did you find your way home?

date

date

date

ECCLESIASTES 11:1-2

Send out your bread upon the waters,
for after many days you will get it back.
Divide your means seven ways, or even eight,
for you do not know what disaster may happen on earth.

date

What does it mean to "send out your bread upon the waters? How have you done this? How did or does it return to you?

date

ECCLESIASTES 11:5

Just as you do not know how the breath comes to the bones in the mother's womb, so you do not know the work of God, who makes everything.

date

Modern science answers some of life's mysteries, but certainly not all. What mysteries exist for you, be they the ways of life or the ways of God? What urgent questions do you have for God?

date

date

date

ECCLESIASTES 11:8-10

Even those who live many years should rejoice in them all, yet let them remember that the days of darkness will be many. All that comes is vanity.

Rejoice, young man, while you are young, and let your heart cheer you in the days of your youth. Follow the inclination of your heart and the desire of your eyes, but know that for all these things God will bring you into judgment.

Banish anxiety from your mind, and put away pain from your body, for youth and the dawn of life are vanity.

date

In these verses, what strikes you as most true in your experience? What strikes you as out of touch with your reality? Reflect on how you deal with anxiety or pain.

date

date

date

ECCLESIASTES 12

Remember your creator in the days of your youth, before the days of trouble come and the years draw near when you will say, "I have no pleasure in them"; before the sun and the light and the moon and the stars are darkened and the clouds return with the rain; in the day when the guards of the house tremble, and the strong men are bent, and the women who grind cease working because they are few, and those who look through the windows see dimly; when the doors on the street are shut, and the sound of the grinding is low, and one rises up at the sound of a bird, and all the daughters of song are brought low; when one is afraid of heights, and terrors are in the road; the almond tree blossoms, the grasshopper drags itself along, and the caper bud falls; because all must go to their eternal home, and the mourners will go about the streets; before the silver cord is snapped, and the golden bowl is broken, and the pitcher is broken at the fountain, and the wheel broken at the cistern, and the dust returns to the earth as it was, and the breath returns to God who gave it.

date

Reflect on what it is about your life that you most appreciate. What will you miss most when the time comes to breathe your last?

date

ECCLESIASTES 12:11-12

The sayings of the wise are like goads, and like nails firmly fixed are the collected sayings that are given by one shepherd. Of anything beyond these, my child, beware. Of making many books there is no end, and much study is a weariness of the flesh.

date

Looking back over the sayings you have read and pondered in the book of Ecclesiastes, which of them would you want to hang on your wall or put on a magnet for your refrigerator?

What do you think of the idea of living by a few simple truths versus expanding your mind by much study?

date

date

date

ECCLESIASTES 12:13-14

The end of the matter; all has been heard. Fear God, and keep his commandments, for that is the whole duty of everyone. For God will bring every deed into judgment, including every secret thing, whether good or evil.

date

As you reflect on Ecclesiastes, what really is the end of the matter for you? How would you summarize life's meaning or purpose? What would you include in a personal mission statement?

date

date

date